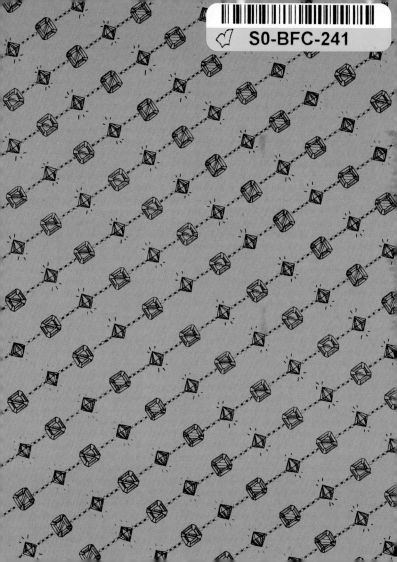

JEWELS

Anne Harvey
Illustrated by Philip Argent

The Leprechaun Library
published by
G.P. PUTNAM'S SONS
NEW YORK

PRECIOUS STONES

Ruby, amethyst, emerald, diamond,
Sapphire, sardonyx, fiery-eyed carbuncle,
Jacynth, jasper, crystal-a-sheen;
Topaz, turquoise, tourmaline, opal,
Beryl, onyx and aquamarine:
Marvel, O mortal! – their hue, lustre, loveliness,
Pure as a flower when its petals unfurl –
Peach-red carnelian, apple-green chrysoprase,
Amber and coral and orient pearl!

WALTER DE LA MARE

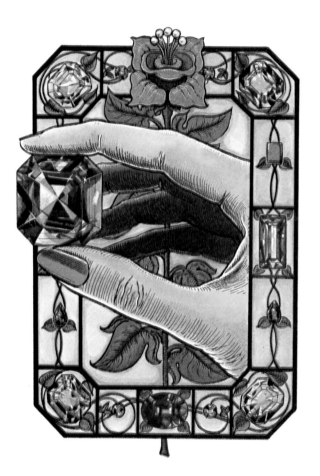

THE JEWEL OF JOY

The reddish-brown carnelian is one of the luckiest jewels to wear. It was said to make its wearer extremely content and, on a more encouraging note, 'No man wearing a carnelian was ever found in a collapsed house or beneath a fallen wall'. Perhaps it would be as popular now as in ancient Babylon and Greece if we still believed in it as a talisman of good luck and joy.

The carnelian is also a jewel which has been closely associated with the Mohammedan peoples. The Prophet Mohammed wore an inscribed carnelian set in a ring, and taught his followers that whoever wore this jewel would never cease to be happy and blessed. Mohammedans still believe that wearing the carnelian will maintain 'their equanimity in provoking situations', be it a violent argument or a hysterical outburst of laughter.

The carnelian's popularity as a good-luck charm was not restricted to the East. In the nineteenth century, Napoleon III had an octagonal-shaped carnelian seal attached to his watch chain, and he hated to be without it. Although wearing this seal did not prevent him from losing his throne, he nevertheless passed it on to his son, the Prince Imperial, who wore it around his neck as his father wished. However, some people believe that the Prince was not wearing it when he met his death at the hands of Zulu warriors while out riding in the South African bush, for the jewel was never recovered from his body.

THE CELESTIAL GEM

The colours of the sapphire – ranging from inky-blue to sky-blue – immediately put one in mind of the sky and, for this reason, early Christian theologians believed that to gaze on the sapphire would elevate a man's thoughts from earthly to heavenly matters. Carrying this connection even further, they speculated that when Moses received the Ten Commandments they must have been written on tablets made of sapphire.

These associations made the sapphire a worthy choice for church jewellery, and a sixth-century Papal Bull ruled that every cardinal must wear a sapphire ring on his right hand – the hand used for blessing. When Bishop Marbodeus praised its virtues six hundred years later it was not clear if it was for these heavenly associations or the belief that the sapphire could control a man's sexual appetite.

One wonderful sapphire, called in French the *'sapphire merveilleux'*, shone curiously blue by day and violet by night. This change in colour in fact depended on the amount of natural light which shone through the jewel. When its owner gave it to his lady, he deceitfully misinformed her that if it turned violet it would be proof of her infidelity, but if it turned blue it would proclaim her pure. The poor woman, ignorant of the real reason why the jewel changed colour, spent many anxious hours watching the jewel. At last the man realized the pain his deception was causing her, and revealed the strange properties of the jewel. He may well have been influenced by the sapphire's reputed power to mend manners.

THE STONE OF SADNESS

From ancient times the onyx has been regarded as an ominous stone. Indeed, in Arabic its name (*el Jaza*) means sadness. Admirers of the onyx are advised therefore to wear the orange stone sard with it, as this stone neutralizes its malignant influence.

In Ancient China, the onyx was so dreaded that some men were afraid even to enter mines in which it might be found, and those who dared to wear it were pronounced to be bereft of their senses. The onyx, they were warned, could lead to terrifying dreams, doubts, disputes and lawsuits.

Wearers of the onyx fared no better in affairs of the heart. Although strikingly beautiful, the black- and white-banded onyx was believed to cool the ardours of love. People thought this was caused by the sharp contrast of the stone's colours, which provoked disagreement and finally separation between lovers.

However, for all its gloomy associations, the onyx could be beneficial to women in childbirth. An onyx described as 'so large that a man could not hold it in his hand' formed part of a shrine to the English martyr St Alban at the country town which later bore his name. It was loaned out to women who were about to give birth. One woman who wanted a large family was so grateful for the benefits she received from the stone that she refused to part with it.

THE KING OF GEMS

According to a Burmese legend the first rubies were hatched from an egg laid deep in the earth by a mysterious serpent. This creature laid three eggs: out of the first egg came the King of Pagan and out of the second the Emperor of China; when the third egg was hatched, the shell broke to reveal the rubies for which the Burmese mines were subsequently famous.

The Hindus called the ruby *Ratnaraj*, or King of Precious Stones. In the case of the ruby, nature for once matches the claims of myth. One magnificent specimen found on the island of Ceylon was the length of a man's palm and the thickness of a man's arm. Many European travellers saw this jewel, among them the thirteenth-century Venetian Marco Polo, who pronounced it 'the most precious article that exists in the world, a glorious and incomparable specimen, free from flaw and red as fire'.

Always prized for its gleaming red colour, men believed that the ruby would shine through even the thickest layers of clothing. They also thought that if the possessor of a fine ruby touched the limits of his property with the jewel his house and land would be protected from storms and lightning.

The Bible says that the price of a virtuous woman is above that of rubies and suggests that such ladies are hard to find. A woman wishing to prove her virtue should try wearing the ruby on her left hand, as this is supposed to control amorous desire.

THE GEM OF BEAUTY

The garnet has always been a popular jewel which, through the ages, has been used in a variety of ways. The ancient Egyptians adored its deep red colour and garnets set into necklets and armlets have often been discovered in their tombs. The garnet also had an explicitly religious significance for the Egyptians. Statues of the powerful goddess Isis incorporated garnets in her ceremonial belt, for the red colour of the stone was believed to represent her blood and therefore her power.

In the seventeenth century, the form of the clear, red gem was likened 'unto the flowers of the pomegranate', but a hundred years later garnets were put to a strange use. When fighting on the Kashmir frontier the Hanza tribe used them instead of bullets, believing that the blood-red stones would inflict a far more grievous wound on their enemies than the common lead bullet. Their adversaries, however, were only too happy to keep the valuable missiles.

Perhaps the real heyday of the garnet was the Victorian era. Ladies of quality proudly displayed matching sets of garnets in earrings, necklaces, bracelets and rings. The dramatic hue of the jewel was felt to be most becoming, and in particular flattering to the complexion. As well as enhancing a woman's beauty, garnets also bestow on the wearer the quality of constancy and the ability to make deep and lasting friendships.

THE JEWEL OF VENUS

Green, the colour of natural things, has long been thought beneficial to sight, and the green emerald was once held to have such strong curative properties that it was considered more use than a pair of spectacles. According to an Indian tale, this sparkling jewel had its origins in the natural world. One night a man saw a very brilliant firefly alight on the grass. However, when he approached to look closer it was not an insect he found but an emerald.

The emerald is most commonly associated with the earth-goddess Venus, to whom it was sacred because its green colour symbolized fertility and growth, two of her main concerns. Moreover, as Venus was the goddess of love, the emerald could also indicate whether or not love was true: 'If faithful, it is like the leaves in spring, / If faithless, like those leaves when withering.'

It is said that a woman should not wear an emerald until she is fifty whereas a man may wear it at any time. However, the thirteenth-century King Bela of Hungary had cause to regret wearing this jewel, with its powers of revealing falsity. One morning, feeling passionate, he went to embrace his wife. With sweet words she appeared to return his love, whereupon the emerald ring on his finger fell into three parts.

THE JEWEL OF THE SUN

The chrysolite, a golden jewel tinged with the subtlest hint of green, has been prized since ancient times. Nowadays it is not considered so precious and may be better known as the peridot or olivine.

The Egyptians first discovered rich deposits of chrysolite on the island of Zeberged, the 'Serpent Isle' in the Red Sea area. The Pharaohs, dazzled by its beauty, coveted the jewel so highly that they set sentries to guard the deposits against robbers. Anxious to preserve the chrysolite for their exclusive use, they would only allow the royal gemcutters in after nightfall to cut the jewel, and then under heavy supervision. It is not surprising that the jewel should also have appealed to the Crusaders, and many chrysolites were plundered, eventually finding their way into European ecclesiastical treasures. The finest chrysolites from this date are still housed in the cathedral at Cologne.

People likened the sparkling golden light of the chrysolite to the sun, and believed that, like the sun, it had the power to dispel dark forces. It was an especially powerful talisman if bound in gold and held in the right hand, in which guise it would put night hags to flight. It was also said that if the jewel was strung on the hair of an ass and worn on the left arm it would rid people of their follies.

THE HEALING STONE

The ancient Babylonians believed that by carving magical symbols on the bloodstone they could foretell the future. This art of inscribing the jewel was revived during the Middle Ages, when the bloodstone was treated with the utmost awe and respect. This was because the red spots speckled through the green stone were thought to be Christ's blood diffusing through the stone. Indeed, some inscribed bloodstones do seem to depict the thorn-crowned head of Christ in such a way that the red spots appear to be trickling from the hair and face.

The bloodstone was also an essential item in sixteenth-century first-aid boxes. One of its supposed medical properties was its ability to cure nose bleeds. Few people use the bloodstone for that purpose today, but it is widely believed in the West Indies that if a bloodstone is placed on a wound the bleeding will stop.

The bloodstone is also known by the alternative name heliotrope, which means 'turn to the sun'. Magicians believed that if the bloodstone were rubbed with the herb heliotrope the wearer of the stone would become invisible. However, when men noticed that the sun's rays shining down on a bloodstone in a bowl of water caused a red reflection, they grew to believe that the jewel had the power to turn the sun blood-red, and hence, to have the power to raise storms.

THE PERSUASIVE JEWEL

A gate is a gemstone formed in the steam cavities of volcanic rocks and is always striped with either wavy, zigzag or straight concentric bands. Sometimes these markings closely resemble the shape of an eye, and in the East Indies 'eye agates' used to be used as charms against the evil eye, or as the eyes of idols.

On one island, such an idol is said to have ensured that the fishermen's nets were always full. But when its eyes mysteriously disappeared one night the fish immediately deserted the waters. With their source of livelihood gone, the islanders were soon close to starvation. It so chanced that one night a small girl caught sight of something sparkling on the ground and, kneeling down, she discovered the idol's agate eyes. No sooner were they returned to the statue than the fish miraculously returned to the waters.

Agate also seems to be a jewel of seduction – and one which favours the man. According to one nineteenth-century reference book, a man armed with an agate should succeed not only in winning the lady of his choice but also easily 'persuade her to succumb to him'. Perhaps this is why the Bretons believed that a girl's virginity could be tested by making her drink powdered agate mixed with beer. If the unfortunate girl could tolerate this mixture she was pronounced impure.

THE JEWEL OF NOBILITY

According to an old French legend the tale of a lovely young maiden explains how the amethyst got its beautiful purple colour. One day a girl called Amethyst was on her way to worship at the shrine of the goddess Diana when suddenly some ferocious tigers sprang out to attack her. What the maiden did not know was that Bacchus, the god of wine, had ruled in a fit of anger that these beasts must devour the first human being they set eyes on. Terrified, Amethyst appealed to Diana to save her and was promptly transformed into a statue of white crystal. Bacchus, seeing how beautiful the girl looked, repented of his anger and poured grape juice all over the statue, turning the white stone into a glowing purple.

From ancient times the colour purple has been associated with nobility. For this reason the amethyst was once valued as highly as the diamond, and was incorporated into the crowns of kings, the jewels of queens and the rings of bishops. Its colour was a perfect foil for their velvet robes.

Nowadays the amethyst is comparatively less valuable, but it is not a jewel to overlook for it has many virtues. The name amethyst actually means 'not drunken', and to wear this jewel means you will stay sober. It can also control evil thoughts, quicken the wit and make men shrewd in business matters. Men especially liked the amethyst because of the belief that it would attract beautiful women to them, although it seems strange that the jewel was also thought to 'quiet sexual passion'.

THE FORTUNE-TELLER'S JEWEL

As the beryl was the jewel connected with the biblical tribe of Gad, the tribe of good fortune, it seems most appropriate that this is the jewel most suited to fortune-telling. From ancient times gipsies, magicians and others endowed with the power of prophecy have gazed into the beryl's magical sphere. However, it seems that only after the seer had recited mysterious incantations over the beryl could the future be read in the sea-coloured crystal.

People often resorted to magicians and gipsies to cure their ills, and it is not surprising to find the beryl was much used medicinally. It was thought especially efficacious in treating eye injuries. For one remedy, the jewel was pulverized in a mortar, the resulting powder sieved and a small amount inserted in the injured eye. In the fourteenth century the beryl was also claimed to be a cure for hiccoughs. For this remedy, the beryl was steeped in water, then removed, and the remaining liquid swallowed by the patient. (Whether this worked any better than the traditional cold key or slap on the back, it is impossible to know.)

Wearers of the beryl will find themselves alert and keen to get down to work. A generally lively stone, it not only quickens the intellect but, according to a nineteenth-century German treatise, the beryl can re-awaken the love between husband and wife.

THE JEWEL OF LIGHT

The topaz, whose name in Sanskrit means the 'yellow stone', is a jewel influenced by the moon. It shines most brightly at night and its powers of ensuring the wearer with long life, beauty and intelligence wax and wane with the phases of the moon. In the thirteenth century one highly prized topaz is said to have given out such a great light at night that prayers could be read by it. A thieving Benedictine monk, 'the greediest creature that ever went on two legs', stole this precious specimen. Though he did not repent of his crime, the monk became afraid that he would be accused of sacrilege and so he threw the topaz into the sea. Neither the monk nor the topaz were ever seen again.

In India the sour and cold taste of the topaz was considered to make it an excellent appetizer and also it was thought to possess revivifying qualities.

A Hindu magician is said to have possessed one such stone which he would loan on occasion. This restorative jewel was requested once by a great rajah during the heat of a battle. The magician took it to the scene of fighting, but while searching for the rajah he was overcome by an evil force and fell, dying, to the ground. As he breathed his last he heard a sorely wounded soldier crying for help. With the last of his strength he threw the topaz to the man, gasping that he must place the gem against his heart. The soldier did so and miraculously lived to tell the tale.

THE GEM OF THE SEA

The pearl, a gift from the sea, stands apart from all other jewels. Prized for its smooth roundness and opaque appearance, its quiet splendour has also made the pearl a symbol of purity.

The question of the pearl's origin has exercised men's imaginations from earliest times. In a Burmese legend, after the God of the Mines had fashioned the diamond as his jewel, he is said to have created the pearl, 'the gem of the sea', for his queen. Pliny, the Roman naturalist, believed that the pearl was formed as a result of the dew of heaven falling into open oyster-shells. The poet and novelist Sir Walter Scott, echoing an ancient belief, described pearls as being formed from 'tears that Naiads wept'.

However, nothing can match the excitement a pearl-fisher feels as he is about to open an oyster plucked from the sea-bed in which he hopes to find a pearl. The pearl-fisher Kino, in John Steinbeck's story *The Pearl*, felt just this excitement when, one day, he saw a very large oyster lying by itself on the sea-bed. As he dived down to bring the shell to the surface its lid opened slightly, giving out a ghostly gleam. Then it closed again. Once he was out of the water, and with beating heart, Kino deftly opened the shell with his knife. 'He lifted the flesh and there it lay, the great pearl, perfect as the moon. It captured the light and refined it, and gave it back in silver incandescence. It was as large as a sea-gull's egg. It was the greatest pearl in the world.'

JEWELS OF THE ZODIAC

The highly skilled Babylonian astronomers devised the twelve signs of the zodiac to represent the twelve equal sub-divisions of the sun's apparent complete annual circuit of the heavens. The Chaldeans, however, were the first to sense a relationship between the zodiac planets and precious gems. Their discovery spread quickly through the ancient world, and soon men were taking care to wear the appropriate zodiac jewel when its planet was in the ascendant. The truly superstitious might have twelve separate rings, one for each zodiac sign, or even a ring combining all twelve jewels.

However, nowadays people usually limit themselves to the stone that is associated with their birth sign.

ARIES	March 21 – April 20	Bloodstone
TAURUS	April 21 – May 20	Sapphire
GEMINI	May 21 – June 20	Agate
CANCER	June 21 – July 21	Emerald
LEO	July 22 – August 21	Onyx
VIRGO	August 22 – September 21	Carnelian
LIBRA	September 22 – October 22	Chrysolite
SCORPIO	October 23 – November 20	Beryl
SAGITTARIUS	November 21 – December 20	Topaz
CAPRICORN	December 21 – January 20	Ruby
AQUARIUS	January 21 – February 20	Garnet
PISCES	February 21 – March 20	Amethyst

JEWELS AND ANNIVERSARIES

One old tradition that is still universally popular today is that of linking jewels with wedding anniversaries. Early anniversaries are associated with relatively commonplace materials. The first anniversary, for example, is celebrated with a gift of paper, the second with cotton and the third leather. Only when they have been married for twelve years may a couple say it with jewels.

The jewel-linked anniversaries are:

Twelfth anniversary	Agate
Thirteenth anniversary	Moonstone
Seventeenth anniversary	Amethyst
Eighteenth anniversary	Garnet
Thirtieth anniversary	Pearl
Thirty-fifth anniversary	Coral
Fortieth anniversary	Ruby
Forty-fifth anniversary	Sapphire
Fifty-fifth anniversary	Emerald
Sixtieth anniversary	Diamond

JEWELS AND DREAMS

From ancient times, people have sought to interpret their dreams, and to dream of jewels was believed to be of great significance.

The meaning of jewel dreams could be found in books called lapidaries, for in these all the magical and mysterious properties of jewels were set down. A lapidary would reveal, for example, that if a woman dreamt of jewels – especially the beryl – it could result in marriage, pregnancy and the acquisition of wealth. For a man to dream of precious stones was less auspicious unless he happened to be of royal blood: if a king dreamt of red jewels it meant joy, great fortune and increased power, but to dream of blue stones presaged the loss of his kingdom.

Some jewels seemed to change their daytime characteristics by night. For instance, the usually unlucky onyx could foretell a happy marriage, whereas to dream of the virtuous sapphire could foretell a stormy period ahead.

Indeed the interpretations still hold good today. Unlucky jewels include the carnelian, which brings misfortune; the moonstone, which spells danger; and the black jet, which prophesies sorrow. However, for friendship, safety, hope and prosperity try to dream of pearls, amethysts, emeralds and turquoise.

And to avoid dreaming altogether, try wearing a diamond while you sleep.

DIAMONDS ARE A GIRL'S BEST FRIEND

In the nineteenth century, Solly Joel made the very pertinent observation that as long as women are born diamonds will be worn. The burden of buying diamonds, however, does always seem to fall on men and it has been suggested that a man will probably buy three diamonds in his life: one for his wife-to-be; the second for his mistress; and the third for his wife when she finds out about his mistress.

The diamond is the jewel most often associated with sophisticated and glamorous women. The romantic, though very clear-sighted, heroine of Anita Loos's novel *Gentlemen Prefer Blondes* insisted that though a man kissing your hand 'may make you feel very, very good, a diamond bracelet lasts for ever'. Such sentiments are presumably shared by the film star Zsa Zsa Gabor, who is reported to have said that she never hated a man enough to give him his diamonds back.

One would like to think that women were given diamonds as a tribute to their virtue. Unfortunately Mae West, in the film *Diamond Lil*, dispelled any such innocent assumption. Dazzled by the diamonds which adorned Miss West's hour-glass figure, a woman remarked, 'Goodness! What beautiful diamonds!' Miss West was quick to retort, 'Goodness had nothing to do with it, dearie!'

JEWELS AND LOVERS

Although Oscar Wilde said love is 'more precious than emeralds and dearer than fine opals', jewels have always been the supreme token of love. As the English poet Herrick wrote, they are a gift which will endure 'when all your world of Beauty's gone'.

During the heady, romantic days of Elizabeth I it was a popular conceit for the courtier-poet to address his love as 'my own sweet jewel' or 'mine only treasure'. Indeed, few parts of her would escape being likened to gemstones. Her hair might be 'as black as jet', her lips like 'two rubies', her cheeks would be 'of coral' and her teeth likened to 'orient pearls'. One Sir John Harington presented his wife with a diamond ring on the birth of their first son, accompanied by a sonnet in which he described her face as 'unblemished as a clear jewel'.

A lover's gift of jewels could, on the other hand, stand as a reminder of happier times. Indeed, the Empress Josephine derived cold comfort from the jewels given to her by the Emperor Napoleon. When sitting for a portrait, and knowing that her husband was about to divorce her, she chose to wear the jewels she had worn at her last public appearance as the Emperor's wife. She is said to have wistfully told the artist Isabey: 'I am about to change my state ... Paint me in emeralds to represent the undying freshness of my grief, but let them be surrounded with diamonds, to portray the purity of my love.'

VI

L'AMOUREUX.

ALADDIN AND THE JEWEL TREES

Long ago in China lived a boy called Aladdin, the son of a poor widow. One day an evil sorcerer appeared on their doorstep and tricked Aladdin into believing that he was his long-lost uncle. In fact, the magician needed a boy small enough to climb down into a cave to fetch him up a magic lamp.

However, Aladdin was ignorant of this, and only too glad to carry out the request of his new-found uncle. On descending into the cave, he was immediately dazzled by a forest of wondrous trees whose branches were hung with luscious-looking fruits, glistening red, white, green and blue. The boy, too unworldly to know that these were rubies, diamonds, emeralds and sapphires, stuffed them into his pocket intending to eat them later.

He soon found the lamp but he found it hard to ascend as the jewels weighed him down. As he made his slow progress up out of the cave the magician grew impatient, then angry, and finally slammed fast the door of the cave.

Trapped, the terrified boy began to cry. As he did so, his sleeve accidentally rubbed against the lamp. At this a genie appeared and asked Aladdin, 'What are your wishes?' His first wish was to go home. This was immediately granted. He then asked the genie why the fruit he had put in his pocket was so heavy, whereupon the genie told Aladdin that these were no ordinary fruits but fabulous jewels which would make him rich and famous.

From that day on, the troubles of Aladdin and his mother were over. They lived in great wealth and happiness with the genie of the lamp as their protector.

ADAPTED FROM 'THE ARABIAN NIGHTS'

CHARLEMAGNE'S DIAMOND

While living in Zurich, the Emperor Charlemagne set up a bell to be rung by any of his people who had a grievance. One day it rang, and the ringer turned out to be a serpent. Charlemagne followed it to its nest, and saw that a bulging toad had eaten all the serpent's eggs. He condemned the toad to death, and the next day, in gratitude, the serpent brought Charlemagne the most enormous diamond.

This was no ordinary jewel, however, for it conferred upon the giver a lifelong devotion, amounting almost to madness, to the jewel's recipient.

Charlemagne gave the diamond to Fastrada, his fourth wife. Although formerly he had had no great love for her, he now found that he could not leave her side. She, however, recognized the jewel's power, and when she caught a deadly fever she placed the jewel in her mouth just before she died. Charlemagne could not be drawn away from her corpse. At last, Charlemagne's bishop, Turpin, solved the problem by taking the diamond from Fastrada's mouth. Now the gem's power was with him and Charlemagne would not leave his side. Turpin escaped and cast the diamond into a lake, thus freeing himself from the enchantment.

Charlemagne now became strangely restless. Riding out one day he came by this lake into which Turpin had thrown the diamond. There he stopped and could not move, for the diamond still exerted its force through the waters of the lake. He immediately ordered a palace to be built there, and this was the foundation of the city of Aix-la-Chapelle (now Aachen), where Charlemagne was later buried.

THE NECKLACE

Mme Loisel, the pretty and charming wife of a clerk at the Ministry of Justice in Paris, resented the fact that she had not been rich and highly born. She craved expensive clothes and costly jewels and envied all who had them.

One day her husband M. Loisel brought home an invitation to a Ministry party. His wife immediately complained that she had nothing to wear and so he gave her money for a new dress. But this did not satisfy her, for she still had no jewels to wear. Ever patient, M. Loisel suggested that she borrow from her friend Mme Forestier, who had a fine collection of jewels. This she did and after much deliberation she settled for a sparkling diamond necklace.

Mme Loisel outshone all the other women at the party, and returned home jubilant. However, the couple were then horror-struck to discover that the necklace had slipped from her neck and was nowhere to be found. The next day, in great despair, they borrowed 36,000 francs to buy an almost identical necklace, and gave it to Mme Forestier without mentioning their misfortune.

But their troubles did not end there, for the money had to be repaid. So they dismissed their servant, M. Loisel took on evening work, and Mme Loisel worked like a slave, doing any menial work available, in order to save money. After ten long years the money was finally repaid but the effort had aged the couple and made them bitter.

One Sunday, Mme Loisel chanced to meet Mme Forestier again, and the latter hardly recognized her. Mme Loisel explained why she looked so worn and ill, and her old friend was horrified. She told her that the necklace had been made of paste, and was worth only about 5,000 francs.

ADAPTED FROM A SHORT STORY BY GUY DE MAUPASSANT

THE HAPPY PRINCE

Long ago the statue of the Happy Prince stood on a column high above the city. It seemed glorious to the townspeople but they did not notice the huge tears which trickled from his blue sapphire eyes down on to his clothes, made of gold-leaf, and on to the red ruby that gleamed on his sword's hilt.

However, a passing swallow saw that the statue was unhappy. The Prince told him that this was because of all the ugliness and misery he could see in the town around him. The swallow agreed to help him. Taking the red ruby, the bird gave it to a poor dressmaker and her sick son. The bird then took one sapphire to a hungry writer in a garret, and the other to a small, shivering matchgirl.

When the swallow told the Prince that there was still poverty and unhappiness the Prince, blind without his jewelled eyes, asked him to remove all of this gold-leaf clothing and distribute it among the poor.

This the swallow did. But by now winter had come and as the swallow had not left for a warmer climate it was soon frozen with cold. The little bird kissed the Prince on the lips, then fell dead at his feet – at which the Prince's leaden heart broke in two.

The Mayor, now disgusted by the statue's shabbiness, ordered it to be burnt. But the Prince's leaden heart would not melt, so it was thrown on the dust heap with the dead swallow.

When God asked an angel to bring Him the two most precious things from earth, the angel took the bird and the Prince's heart up to the Garden of Paradise where they have remained for ever more.

ADAPTED FROM OSCAR WILDE

PEARLS OF WISDOM

The pearl has symbolized wisdom from earliest times. Yet a pearl, like wisdom, is not always an easy thing to acquire, as the English poet Dryden warns: 'Errors, like straws, upon the surface flow./ He who would search for pearls must dive below.' However, for all this sage advice, a Yiddish proverb seems to suggest that too much wisdom is not a good thing, for 'pearls around the neck are like stones upon the heart'.

The Bible also reminds us not to cast our pearls before swine. But a teacher, Irwin Edmain, freely adapting this sentiment many centuries later, wrote that as far as he was concerned education was 'the process of casting false pearls before real swine'.

One such 'false pearl' might be the recipe suggested by the seventeenth-century writer William Salmon in his book *Polygraphices*. For 'An Incomparable Cosmetick of Pearl' he suggests you should: 'Dissolve pearls in juice of lemons or distilled vinegar digested in horse dung until they send forth a clear oil which will swim on the top.' Salmon advised his readers that this excellent beautifier was well worth £7 an ounce!

JEWELS AND THIEVES

History abounds with gripping and often exciting accounts of jewel robberies. One of the most audacious was Captain Blood's attempt in 1671 to steal the British Crown Jewels from the Tower of London. More surprising perhaps is the fact that at this time these irreplaceable jewels should have been stored in an ordinary locked cupboard.

Over a short period of time Blood, who had disguised himself as a clergyman, ingratiated himself with the Keeper of the Jewels until the deceived man agreed to show them to 'Parson' Blood. When he brought them out, Blood and his two associates drew their rapiers, stabbed the Keeper and made off with the crown, sceptre and orb. Fortunately the villains were soon apprehended and the jewels, which they had dropped on the banks of the Thames, recovered. King Charles II rather admired this adventurer and pardoned his treasonable crime. He also inexplicably awarded him an annual pension of £500 and an estate in Ireland!

However, stealing jewels is not the exclusive prerogative of men; the magpie is notorious for stealing glittering gems. In 'The Jackdaw of Rhiems', a poem by Richard Barham Harris, an acquisitive jackdaw cannot resist the Cardinal of Rhiems's beautiful turquoise ring. When the Cardinal removes it from his finger and puts it to one side, the little jackdaw straightaway flies down and makes off with the ring in his beak.

He hides it in his nest in the belfry, but when the Cardinal brings down terrible curses on the as yet unidentified thief, the guilty jackdaw hops forward. The contrite bird leads the Cardinal and his attendants to the jewel's hiding-place, and henceforth the jackdaw becomes a reformed character.

SHAKESPEARE AND JEWELS

Shakespeare uses jewels in a myriad of ways to conjure up in his audience's mind images of beauty, love, greed, treachery and death.

To the love-sick Romeo the beauty of Juliet appears to hang upon 'the cheek of night / Like a rich jewel in an Ethiop's ear'. After murdering his wife Desdemona, the grief-stricken Othello likens her perfection to 'one entire and perfect chrysolite'. The incurably romantic Orlando in *As You Like It* nails love poems to trees, one of which describes his love Rosalind in the following terms: 'From the east to Western Ind/ No jewel is like Rosalind.'

Shylock, the rich Jew in *The Merchant of Venice,* is driven to distraction when his daughter Jessica elopes, taking with her not only his gold ducats but his two most precious jewels: a wonderful diamond, and a turquoise which he would not have parted with for a 'wilderness of monkeys'. In *Hamlet*, the treacherous King Claudius tries to tempt his stepson, Hamlet, to drink a poisoned draught by dropping a pearl into the goblet and proposing the double-edged toast, 'Here's to thy health.'

Perhaps Shakespeare's most vivid reference to jewels is the Duke of Clarence's prophetic dream in *Richard III*, in which the imprisoned duke dreams of death through drowning. In his dream, he sees on the seabed:

> . . . A thousand men that fishes gnaw'd upon;
> Wedges of gold, great anchors, heaps of pearl,
> Inestimable stones, unvalu'd jewels, . . .
> Some lay in dead men's skulls, and in those holes
> Where eyes did once inhabit, there were crept
> As 'twere in scorn of eyes, reflecting gems.

Immediately after describing this dream the unfortunate duke is drowned in a butt of malmsey wine.

JEWELS OF THE HOURS

Alchemists dabbling in the mysterious curative and protective properties of jewels discovered that they could reveal much about a man's physical and mental development. They also found that these objects of light and colour, formed deep within the earth, could, if used at the right time of day, month or season, enrich a man's spirit.

In the sixteenth century it became fashionable to connect certain jewels with the rhythm of the year: the emerald with spring; the ruby with summer; the sapphire with autumn; and the icy, sparkling diamond with winter. Gems were likewise accorded to the hours of the day, each of the daytime and night-time hours being governed by a jewel.

The jewels of the day, from 7 am through to 6 pm, are chrysolite; amethyst; kunzite; sapphire; garnet; diamond; jacinth; emerald; beryl; topaz; ruby and opal.

The jewels of the night, from 7 pm through to 6 am, are sardonyx; chalcedony; jade; jasper; loadstone; onyx; morion hematite; malachite; lapis-lazuli; turquoise and tourmaline.

ACKNOWLEDGEMENTS

Precious Stones by Walter de la Mare is reprinted by kind permission of the Literary Trustees of Walter de la Mare and the Society of Authors as their representatives.

Of the many books which have provided source material for *Jewels* the most valuable were:

The Magic of Jewels and Charms, G.F. Kunz (London, 1915)
The Curious Lore of Precious Stones, G.F. Kunz (London, 1915)
The History and Mystery of Precious Stones, W. Jones (London, 1880)
Gems, Mab Wilson (London 1965)

Designed and produced for G.P. Putnam's Sons by
Bellew & Higton Publishers Ltd
19-21 Conway Street, London W1P 6JD

Published on the same day in Canada by Academic Press
Canada Limited, Toronto
Library of Congress Catalog Number 81-81026
ISBN 0 399 12663 5
Printed in England
First American Edition 1981

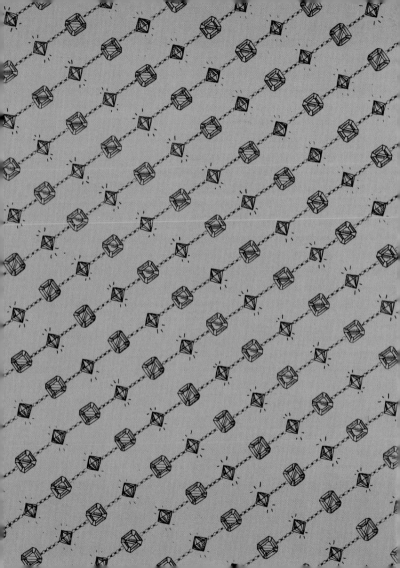